THE POWER *of* GOD'S WORD

Psalm 91 Blessings, Promises, Love Letter

BRYAN HINES

ISBN 979-8-88685-246-2 (paperback)
ISBN 979-8-88685-247-9 (digital)

Copyright © 2022 by Bryan Hines

All rights reserved. No part of this publication may be reproduced, distributed, or transmitted in any form or by any means, including photocopying, recording, or other electronic or mechanical methods without the prior written permission of the publisher. For permission requests, solicit the publisher via the address below.

Christian Faith Publishing
832 Park Avenue
Meadville, PA 16335
www.christianfaithpublishing.com

Printed in the United States of America

THE POWER OF WORDS

In the beginning, God created, or gave birth to, the world and all that is in and on this earth as we know it.

God our Father spoke into existence the plants, trees, seas, insects, reptiles, sun, moon, light, stars by name. Let us go to Genesis 1:1, which says, "In the beginning [time], God [Father] created the Heavens [space] and the Earth [matter]." That was in the New English Translation (NET). In the new Amplified Bible, it says, "In the beginning, God [Elohim] created [by forming from nothing] the heavens and the earth."

Now let us go to John 1:1 (NET), which says, "In the beginning was the word [grace], and the word [grace] was with God, and the word [grace] was fully God."

In the AMP, it states, "In the beginning [before all time] was the word [Christ], and the *word [Christ] was God Himself* [emphasis mine]."

John 1:3 (NET) says, "*All things* were created by Him [God], and apart from Him, not one thing was created that has been created. John 1:3 (AMP) states, "All things were made and came into existence through Him, and without Him [God], not even one thing was made that has come into being."

The power of words, God's Word, is established in heaven and on the earth. When the Father speaks, everybody listens to the Father.

Now Jesus and God (Jehovah) are the same. So when you read the Bible, the recorded Word of God, only believe.

I would like to make a statement about right now. *God does not lie.* Now that I got that off my chest, let us go to the Bible about the *power of words*.

In Matthew 8:5–10 (NET), verse 7 states, "Jesus said to Him [centurion], 'I will come and heal him.' The centurion [a Roman officer] replied, 'Lord, I am not worthy to have you come under my roof. Instead, just say the word and my servant will be healed.' When Jesus heard this, he was amazed and said to those who followed Him, 'I tell you the truth, I have not found such faith in anyone in Israel.'" The key word is *say*.

In Luke 7:1–10 (AMP), verse 7 says, "Therefore I did not even consider myself worthy to come to you, but just *speak* a word and my slave will be healed." The power of words—just *say* or *speak* the word, and you put into action the nature of God Almighty. You honor Him. Now go to Hebrews 4:12 (New King James Version), for this is a *key* to God's Word.

This is my first piece of the great understanding of what God gave me. I will go to Hebrews 4:12 (AMP), which says, "For the word of God is *living* and *active* and full of power [making it operative, energizing, and effective]. It is sharper than any two-edged sword, penetrating as far as the division of the soul and spirit [the completeness of a person] and of both joints and marrow [the deepest parts of our nature], exposing and judging the very thoughts and intentions of the heart. God's word is so powerful, His word can and does change everything around you [italics mine]."

The power of words—the Father's Word (listen to what the Father said)—are mine through Christ my Lord. We must retrain our thinking to kingdom thinking. I am not the same as others (born again) but different through the Father, for He lives in me. I (we) have the mind of Christ in me (us) as long as I/we read the Father's Word. The power of words is very important to your walk with Christ.

God does not lie! The power of the Father's words is yours. They (His words) belong to you, for the Father (God) lives in you. When you received the Christ as your Savior, you opened the storehouse of heaven; and God the Father, God the Son, and God the Holy Spirit moved in. Why? Because you and I were bought with one drop of blood from Emmanuel's side. You are of the household of God. Always remember this and say or speak God's word. Then watch God work in the law of the spirit.

When the Father's word leaves your mouth, you are giving birth to His words. Speaking a miracle, healing, blessings—the word will never come back void, but the word will accomplish what the word was set out to do.

Now Proverbs 30:5 (NET) says, "Every word of the Father [God] is purified; He is like a shield for those who take refuge in Him." See also Psalm 91.

The point is that God's word is trustworthy; it has no defects or flaws, and nothing is false or misleading.

Psalm 12:6 (NET) says, "The Lord's words are absolutely reliable. They are as untainted as silver purified in a furnace on the ground, where it is thoroughly refined." Read also Psalm 12:16 (AMP) promises.

Psalm 89:34–35 says, "My covenant *I will not violate*, nor will *I alter the utterance of my lips*. Once [for all] I have sworn by my holiness [my vow which cannot be violated]; I will not lie to David." I will not lie to my children, which is the body of Christ, the firstborn. *The Father does not lie.*

When the Father spoke the world and all that is in the earth, it was by His power of His word that everything came into existence.

The Father's word is established in heaven and on the earth. The Father's word will never be altered. What He said, *He meant*. And will He not do what He said? Yes, remember *God cannot lie*.

Now go to Proverbs 4:20–22 in the New King James Version. It says, "My son [Bryan] give [pay] attention to my word; [listen to your Father's word] incline your ear to my sayings [word]. Do not let them [my words] depart from your eyes; keep them [my words] in the midst [center] of your heart [spirit]; for they [my words] are life [treasure] to those who find them [treasure hunt], and healing to all their flesh."

A thought, unspoken, will die unborn. God's word spoken will give birth and/or life. This is the power of the Father's words.

Now go to Hebrews 1:3, 4 (AMP), which states, "The son is the radiance and only *expression of the glory* of [our awesome] *God* [reflecting God's shekinak glory, the light being, the brilliant light of the divine], and *the exact representation and perfect imprint of His*

Father's essence, and upholding and maintaining and propelling *all things* [the entire physical and spiritual universe] by *His powerful word* [carrying the universe along to its predetermined goal]. When He [himself and no other] had [by offering Himself on the cross as a sacrifice for sin] accomplished purification from sins and established our freedom from guilt, He (Jesus) sat down [revealing His completed work] at the right hand of the Majesty on High [revealing His divine authority], having become as much superior to angels since He has *inherited* a more excellent and glorious name (Jesus) than they (angels) [that is, son—the name above all names]," Jesus. Read Philippians 2:9 and Ephesians 2:6.

The power of words—life and death, praise or condemnation, to edify or to tear down—that's what you have in your mouth. Look at Proverbs 6:2 (NKJV). It says, "You [Bryan] are snared [entangled] by the words of your mouth [utterance of your lips]; you [Bryan] are taken by the words of your mouth [caught by the words you have spoken]."

Basically, what you say is what you get. Confession brings possession; possession brings your words into reality. You are calling the spiritual laws into motion. You can touch your words.

So you see, the power of words is very important to your walk with Christ. Retrain your thinking to speak the word of God only.

You will become a river of living water that comes out of your spirit. You are a delegate, you are a representative, you are an ambassador, you are a lawyer, you are His (the Father's) son/daughter, joint heir to Jesus. You are sitting at the right hand of God through Christ (Ephesians 2:6 AMP).

Look at Galatians 2:20, which states, "I have been crucified with Christ [that is, in Him I have shared His crucifixion]; it is no longer I who live, but Christ lives in me. The life I now live in the body I live by faith [by adhering to, relying on, and completely trusting] in the Son of God [Jesus], who loves me and gave himself up for me."

Also see Ephesians 2:6–7, which says, "And He [God] raised us [the body] up together with Him [when we believed], and seated us with Him in the heavenly places, [because we are] in Christ Jesus, [and He did this] so that in the age to come He might [clearly] show the immeasurable and unsurpassed riches of His grace in [His] kindness toward us in Christ Jesus [by providing for our redemption]."

This is who you are. You have what the Bible says about you, and you can do what the power of God's word says you can do. We are the *body of Christ*. That means the body can go into the presence of God the Father with the same confidence and assurance that the head can! Boldly! We are sons and daughters of God. We are joint heirs with Jesus Christ. We are *covenant people*. We have a *legal right*, a gospel right, a son and daughter's right, a family right, a body to enter the throne room.

The Father's Word can invoke, decree, and restrain order on Satan and his demons.

Bind and loose Matthew 18:18 (NKJV) power of words this belongs to us (this is ours) His body, also the power of the Father's words, we speak.

Brothers and sisters, you have the mind of Christ. That's the Father's Word. Read 1 Corinthians 2:16 (mind), 2 Corinthians 4:4 (image), 2 Corinthians 11:31 (not lying), and 1 Peter 1:3 (mind ready).

In order to cultivate (develop, improve, nourish, discipline, rethank), you must read God's Word daily. Open the Father's Word, the Holy Bible, and see who you are, what you have, and what you can do in God's Word, His power.

Remember you are born into God's family (household), joint heirs with Christ. Romans 8:17 (AMP) states, "And if [we are His] children, [then we are His] heirs also: *heirs of God* and fellow heirs with Christ [sharing His spiritual blessing and inheritance], if indeed we share in His suffering so that we may also share in His glory [italics mine]." I have shared.

Here are some more scriptures: 1 Peter 1:4, John 1:12, Matthew 25:24, Galatians 13:29, Colossians 1:2, and Colossians 13:24. I like what the Amplified Bible says about these verses. That is my opinion. You can look them up for yourself.

When I asked Jesus into my life, I was twenty-five years old. The Father had me read Hebrews 4:12 (NKJV), and He said, "This is yours, my son. The scripture is a key to open doors to heaven and on earth. For the Word of God is living [active, anointed, working] and powerful [effective, quick, swift, in control, omnipotent] and sharper than any two-edged sword, piercing even to division of soul and spirit, joints and marrow, and is a discerner of the thoughts and intents of the heart."

The Father said to me, "*Do you remember*, my word is established in heaven and on the earth. My word will never change. I meant what I said."

The Father does not lie.

That is why you (us, the body) must speak the word of God. Hold on to God's word and remind Him (the Father) of what he said. *Praise him* and *glorify the Father* after every time you talk to God. *Tell Him you love Him, always praise*, no matter what the world wants to throw at you.

You live in the world, but you are not of this world. You are a citizen of heaven. The Father's kingdom and household of God. Jesus, who is God, said, "I have overcome the world." And so have I, for Christ lives in me! God's word is established in heaven and on the earth. It is like a blank check that someone gives you and says, "Write the amount, it is yours. Better yet, when you find the *truth*, the *treasure*, the truth will set you free!"

I hunted buried treasure when I was younger, and I looked for clues to help me along the way.

So when I asked Jesus into my life, I started to read the King James Version. It was hard for me to read, so I asked Janice (my wife) to buy the New American Standard Bible for me. Which she did for my first Easter as a citizen and in Christ. Then I began to look for clues to God in His Word, and to my eyes, I could see the Father all throughout the Bible. Then I noticed the power of His words, blessings, promises, and a love letter to His children. I learned that when God speaks, everyone and everything listens. I mean all things listen because the Father created all things, and He gave everything to the Son (John 16:12–22)—the firstborn of many sons and daughters, Jesus.

The Father showed me who I am, what I can do, and what I have in the Father's Word. I have been told there are over three thousand promises in the Bible. I don't know, but with me, as a treasure hunter, it would be great to find them all. I have found—or should I say the Holy Spirit revealed—some of the three thousand promises.

So let's go on a treasure hunt of the power of God's Word. *God does not lie.* That is our foundation to the hunt.

Remember, you are born into God's family (the household of God), and we are joint heirs with Christ. We are Christ's body on the earth. Romans 8:17 states, "Now if we are children, then we are heirs—heirs of God and co-heirs with Christ, if indeed we share in his sufferings in order that one may also in his glory."

Here are scriptures you can look up about yourself in the body: 1 Peter 1:4, John 1:12, Matthew 25:34, Galatians 3:29 (key verse), and Colossians 1:12, 3:24. God's word is established in heaven and on the earth. God's word will never change. God meant what he said. We must speak the Father's word and watch. God does not lie!

The power of words in Ephesians 4:29 (NKJV) states, "Let no corrupt communication proceed out of your mouth, but what is good for necessary edification [building up], that it may impart grace to the hearers."

Ephesians 4:29 (AMP) says, "Do not let unwholesome [foul, profane, worthless, vulgar] words ever come out of your mouth, but only such speech as in good for building up others. According to the need and the occasion, so that it will be a blessing to those who hear [you speak]."

This is one that "I don't have to see, I know." It's the story of the centurion in Matthew 8:5–10 and Luke 7:1–10. You can read this; it is great faith. The centurion recognized the authority that Christ had. He might have seen it (Christ at work) or heard it; I do not know. But this I do know. He (the centurion) believed Jesus could heal his servant from dying.

I don't have to see. I know!

In the Old Testament, Esau sold his birthright, by *his own words*, for food (Genesis 25:31–34).

In Deuteronomy 28:1–15 (promised, blessing for obedience) and Deuteronomy 28:16–68 (promised, curses for disobedience), you may read for yourself. I don't know about you, but when I read the Bible, God's holy Word, I love the blessing and promises. It is like a love letter to us, His children.

This body must obey God's Word, for there is power in His words. We are delegates for Jesus; we have been sent by God.

Jesus is the image of God, the exact (clue) *imprint of the father*. To see this imprint, go to John 10:30, 38 (NKJV). "I and my Father are one…but if I do it, though you do not believe me, believe the works, that you may know and believe that the Father is in me, and I in him." You can say everything the Father said. Why? Jesus and God are one and the Holy Spirit.

Now listen to John 14:10 in the Amplified Bible. "Do you not believe that I am in the Father, and the Father is in me? The words I say to you I do not say on my own initiative or authority, but the Father, abiding [living] continually in me, *does his works* [his attesting miracles and acts of power]."

Here is a key to binding and loosing.

Ephesians 1:15–23 and 2:1, 6 (NKJV) state the following:

> Therefore I [Paul] also, after I heard of your faith in the Lord Jesus and your love for all the saints, I [Paul] do not cease to give thanks for you [Bryan] making mention of you [Bryan] in my prayers: that the God of our Lord Jesus Christ, the Father of Glory, may give to you [Bryan] the spirit of wisdom and revelation in the knowledge of him [God], the eyes of your understanding being enlightened; that you [Bryan] may know *what is* the hope of His calling *what are* the riches of the glory of his inheritance in the saints, and *what is* the exceeding greatness of His power toward us *who believe*, according to the working of His mighty power which He [God] worked in Christ when He [God] raised Him [Jesus] from the dead and seated Him [Christ] at his right hand in the heavenly places [overcome] *far above all* principality [rule] and power [authority] and

might [power] and dominion, and *every name that is named*, not in this age, but also in that which is to come. And He [God] put *all* things under His [Jesus] feet and gave Him [Christ] to be head over *all* things to the church [Jesus's body], which is His body, the fullness of Him [God] who fills all in all. You he made alive, who were dead in trespasses and sin and raised us [the body] up together, and made us sit together in the heavenly places in Christ Jesus [italics mine].

This is a prayer (one of many) for the body of Christ, and you (we) can pray the same. Pray for yourself. It is true. I have prayed this prayer of Paul's, and it changed my life. I know this prayer will change your life.

So read Ephesians 3:14–21. This is a prayer of realization for the church, the body of Christ Jesus:

> For this reason, I [Paul] bow my knees to the father of one Lord Jesus Christ, from whom the whole family in Heaven and Earth is name, that he [God] would grant you [Bryan] according to the riches of His *glory* to be strengthened with might through His spirit in the inner man, that Christ may dwell in your heart [spirit] through faith, that you [Bryan] being rooted and grounded in love [compassion], may be able to comprehend with all the saints *what is the width* and *length* and *depth* and *heights* to know the love of Christ which passes knowledge; that you [Bryan] may be filled with *all* [all, all, all] the fulness of God. Now to Him [God] who is able *to do exceedingly, abundantly above all* that we ask or think accordingly to the power that works in us, to him [God] be glory in the church by Christ

Jesus throughout *all* ages, world without end [italics mine]. Amen.

Every word is true in the two prayers that come from God's Word. They are very powerful as you read them out loud. When you read God's Word out loud, you are telling the devil, "This is what my Father has promised me." And at the same time, you are reminding the Father what He said or promised. You are putting the spiritual law in action.

There is one more prayer I would like you to read, and that is in Colossians 1:9–14, a prayer from Paul to/for the Colossians and/or the body of Christ:

> For this reason, we [Paul and Timothy] also, since the day we heard it, do not ease to pray for you [Bryan] and to ask that you [Bryan] may be *filled* with the knowledge of His [God] will [kingdom thanking] in *all wisdom* and *spiritual* understanding; that you [Bryan] have a walk worthy of the Lord, fully pleasing Him [God, Father], being fruitful in every good work and increasing in the knowledge of God, strengthened with all might, according to His glorious power, for all patience and longsuffering with joy; giving thanks to the *Father who has qualified us to be partakers* of the inheritance of the saints in the light. He [God, Father] has delivered us from the power of darkness and translated (transferred) us into the kingdom of the son of His love, *in whom* [italics mine] we have redemption [kingdom thinking] through his blood, the forgiveness of sins [one drop of blood].

These are three prayers Paul wrote for the church (His body). This is the power of words from God that is here for us today. These three prayers changed my life forever.

Here are some more prayers you can look up for yourself: 2 Thessalonians 1:11–12 (prayer of blessing), Ephesians 6:18–20 (prayer for boldness), John 17:20–26 (prayer for all believers), 1 John 5:14, 15 (prayer for guidance), Philip 1:3–11 (prayer for love), 1 Corinthians 1:4–9, Philippians 1:4–7, and Colossians 1:3–8 (prayer of thanksgiving).

The Father does not change. The Father does not conform to the word or anything He spoke into existence. *The Father wants us to return to Him.* God is not like us humans. He is superior to all things. We need to *repent and return* to the Father. This is what the Father wants the church/body to do today (right now). Draw near to Him (God), and God will draw near to you (us, His children). Get off the couch, go to church, fellowship with the body of believers, and listen to God talking to you. Do not judge other people; they have to carry their own cross, not you. Take care of your own self. That's a full-time job. (Thank you, JD.) Always remember, the Holy Spirit is here to guide you into all truths and lead you.

I said there must be something more? James 1:17 (AMP) states, "Every good thing given and every perfect gift is from above; it comes down from the Father of light [the creator and sustainer of the heavens] *in whom* [italics mine] there is no variation [no rising or setting] or shadow cast by his turning [for He is perfect and never changes]."

So every good thing given and every perfect gift is from the Father through His words. I liked that, so I went to Proverbs 9:10 to know God's wisdom, knowledge, and understanding.

Proverbs 9:10 (NET) says, "The beginning of wisdom is to fear the Lord, and acknowledging the Holy one is understanding."

Proverbs 2:1–6 (NET) states the following:

> My child, if you receive my words and store up my commands [treasure my commands] within you, by making your ear attentive to wisdom, and by turning your heart to understanding, indeed, if you call out for discernment—raise your voice for understanding—if you seek it like silver, and search for it like *hidden treasure*, then

you will understand how to fear the Lord, and you will discover knowledge about God. For the Lord gives wisdom, and from his mouth comes knowledge and understanding.

The power of God's words for wisdom, knowledge, and understanding are in the Holy Bible, the written Word of God. Trust in what the Father says about you with all your heart every single day.

Proverbs 3:5, 6 (NET) says, "Trust in the Lord with all your heart and do not rely on your own understanding. Acknowledge him in all your ways, and He will make your paths straight."

Proverbs 3:13, 14 (AMP) states, "Happy [blessed, considered fortunate, to be admired] is the man who finds [skillful and godly] wisdom, and the man who gains understanding and insight [learning from God's word and life's experiences], for wisdom's profit is better than the profit of silver, and her gain is better than fine gold."

The power of God's Word is a treasure that always grows and never ends. The Father's Word, or the power of his words, will change your life forever. *Only believe.* Now listen to the words in Ecclesiastes 7:11, 12 (NET), which states, "Wisdom, like an inheritance, is a good thing; it benefits those who see the light of day. For *wisdom provides protection*, just as money provides protection. But the advantage of knowledge is this: wisdom preserves the life of its owner [italics mine]." This is a key!

Wisdom acknowledges God's orchestration of life. Job 28:28 (NET) states, "And He said to mankind, '*The fear of the Lord—that is wisdom*, and to *turn away from evil is understanding* [italics mine].'"

The New Testament has a scripture that stands out and proclaims in James 1:5 (NET), "But if anyone deficient in wisdom, he should ask God, who gives to all generously and without reprimand, and it [wisdom] will be given to him."

Ephesians 5:15–18 says, "Therefore be very careful how you live—not as unwise but as wise, taking advantage of every opportunity, because the days are evil. For this reason, do not be foolish, but be wise by understanding what *the Lord's will is*, and do not get drunk with wine, which is debauchery, but be filled by the spirit."

This is what God says in his Word—a promise, a blessing, and a love letter to the body of Christ. Here are more scriptures in the Father's words, and they are powerful.

In 2 Chronicles 7:14 (NET), it says, "If my people, who belong to me, humble themselves, pray, seek to please me, and repudiate their sinful practices, then I will respond from heaven, and heal their land."

Jeremiah 18:7–8 says, "There are times, Jeremiah, when I threaten to uproot, tear down, and destroy a nation or kingdom. But if that nation I threatened stops doing wrong, I will cancel the destruction I intended to do it." Nations or kingdoms—repent!

James 1:17 (AMP) states, "Every good thing given and every perfect gift is from above; it comes down from the Father of light [the creator and sustainer of the heavens], *in whom* [italics mine] there is no *variation* [no rising or setting] or shadow cast by his turning [for he, God, is perfect and never changes]."

Hebrews 6:13–30 (International Children's Bible) proclaims, "God made a promise to Abraham, and as there is no one greater than God, he used himself when he swore to Abraham. He [God] said, 'I will surely bless you and give you many descendants.'" Abraham waited patiently for this to happen, and *he received what God promised.*

People always use the name of someone greater than themselves when they swear. The oath proves that what they say is true, and this ends all arguing about what they said. God wanted to prove that His promise was true. He wanted to prove this to those who would get what He promised. He wanted them to understand clearly that *His* purposes never change. So God proved His promise by also making an oath. These two things cannot change. *God cannot lie* (Numbers 23:19, 20; Hebrews 6:18; Titus 1:2) when He makes a promise, and He cannot lie when He makes an oath. These things encourage us who came to God for safety (Psalm 91). They give us strength to hold on to the hope we have been given. We have this hope as an anchor for the soul, sure and strong. It enters behind the curtain in the most holy place in heaven. Jesus has gone in there ahead of us and for us. He has become the priest forever, a priest like Melchizedek.

In 1 Corinthians 3:16–23 (NKJV), it states, "Do you know that you are the temple of God and that the spirit of God dwells in you? If anyone defiles the temple of God, God will destroy him. For the temple of God is holy, which temple are you. (I am holy.) Let no one deceive himself. If anyone among you seems to be wise in this age, let him become a fool that he may become wise. For the wisdom of the world is foolishness with God. One more time, the wisdom of the world is foolishness with God. For it is written, "He catches the wise in their own craftiness." And again it says, "*The Lord knows the thoughts* of the wise, that they are futile." Therefore let no one glory in men. *For all things are yours.* Whether Paul or Apollo or Cephas or the world or life or death or things present or things to come—*all are yours*, and *you are Christ's*, and Christ is God's.

John 16:12–15 says, "I have many more things to say to you, but you cannot bear [to hear] them now. But when He, the spirit of truth, come, He will guide you into all the truth [full and complete truth]. For He [Holy Spirit] will not speak on His own initiative, but He will speak whatever He hears [from the Father—the message regarding the son], and He will disclose to you [Bryan] what is to come [in the future]. He will glorify and honor Me [Jesus] because He (the Holy Spirit) will take from what is mine and will disclose it to you. *All things* that the Father has are mine. Because of this, I said that He [the spirit] will take from what [everything, all things that the Father has] is mine and will *reveal it to you*."

We are His body. That is why Jesus said that *all things—everything* the Father has—is ours. For we are the body of Christ. With that said, here are scriptures on us, His body, the body of Christ. Romans 12:4, 5 (NET) says, "For just as in one body we have many members, and not all the members serve the same function, so we who are many are one body in Christ, and individually, we are members who belong to one another."

In 1 Corinthians 10:17 (AMP), it states, "Since there is one loaf of bread, we [believers] who are many are [united into] one body; for we all partake of the one bread [which represents the body of Christ]."

In 1 Corinthians 12:12, 13, 20 (NET), it says, "For just as the body is one and yet has many members, and all the members of the body—though many—are one body, so too is Christ. For in one spirit we were all baptized into one body, whether Jews or Greeks or slaves or free, we were all made to drink of the one spirit."

In 1 Corinthians 12:20 (AMP), it states, "But now [as things really are] there are many parts [different limbs and organs], but a single body."

In 2 Corinthians 5:10 (AMP), it says, "For we [believers will be called to account and] must all appear before the judgment seat of Christ, so that each one may be repaid for what has been done in the body whether good or bad [that is, each will be held responsible for his actions, purposes, goals, motives—*the use or misuse of his time*, opportunities, and abilities]."

Ephesians 4:4–6, 16 (NET) states, "There is one body [of believers] and one spirit, just as you too were called to the one hope of your calling [to salvation]. One Lord, one faith, one baptism, one God and Father of all, *who is over all and through all and in all*. Amen."

Ephesians 4:16 (NET) says, "From Him the whole body grows, fitted and held together through every supporting ligament. As each one does its part, the body grows in love."

Colossians 3:15 (AMP) states, "Let the peace of Christ [the inner calm of one who walks daily with Him] be the controlling factor in your hearts [deciding and settling questions that arise]. To this peace indeed you were called as members in one body [of believers]. And be thankful [to God always]."

Matthew 18:18, 19, 20 (AMP) states the following:

> I assume you and most solemnly say to you, whatever you bind [forbid, declare to be improper and unlawful] on earth shall have [already] been bound in heaven, and whatever you loose [permit, declare lawful] on earth shall have [already] been loosed in heaven. Again, I say to you that if two believers on earth agree [Amos 3:3—that is, are of one mind, in harmony] about

anything that they ask [within the will of God], it will be done for them by my Father in heaven. For where two or three are gather in my name [meeting together as my followers], I am there among them."

Mark 11:23, 24 (NET) proclaims the following:

I tell you the truth, if someone says to this mountain [problem], "Be lifted up and thrown into the sea," and does not doubt in his heart but *believes that what he says will happen*, it will be done for him. For this reason, I tell you whatever you pray and ask for in prayer [in accordance with God's will] that you have received them, and they will be given to you." (I don't have to see. I know.)

John 14:12–14 (NKJV) says the following:

Most assuredly, I say to you, He [Bryan] who believes in me [Jesus], the work that I do, He [Bryan] will do also; and greater works than these He [Bryan] will do, because I go to the Father and whatever you [Bryan] ask in my name [Jesus], that I will do, that the Father may be glorified in the Son. If you [Bryan] ask *anything* in my name [Jesus], I will do it.

John 15:7 (NKJV) says, "If you [Bryan] abide in me and my words abide in you [Bryan], you [Bryan] will ask what you [Bryan] desire (wish), and it shall be done for you [Bryan]."

James 5:13–16 (NKJV) states as follows:

Is anyone among you suffering? Let him pray. *Is anyone* cheerful? Let him sing psalms.

> *Is anyone* among you sick? Let him call for the elders of the church, and let them pray over him, anointing him with oil in the name of the Lord. And the prayer of faith will save the sick, and the Lord will raise him up, and if he has committed sins, he will be forgiven. Confess your trespasses [sins] to one another, and pray for one another, that you may be healed. The *effective, fervent prayer* of a righteous man avails much.

James 5:19, 20 (NKJV) says, "Brethren, if anyone among you wanders from the truth and someone turns him back, let him know that He who turns a sinner from the error of his way will save a soul from death and cover a multitude of sins."

Psalm 23:5 (NKJV) states, "You [God] prepare a table before me in the presence of my enemies; you [God] anoint my head with oil; my cup runs over." (What's on the table is grace, mercy, love, peace, joy, patience, confidence, righteousness, deliverance, understanding, knowledge, wisdom, armor, and everything you need.)

In 1 Peter 2:9 (NKJV), it says, "But you are a chosen generation, a royal priesthood, a holy nation, his own special people, that you may proclaim the praises of Him who called you out of darkness into His marvelous light." (This is a key to who you are.)

Colossians 1:13 (NET) says, "He delivered us from the power of darkness and transferred us [body] to the kingdom of the Son he loves."

Now Psalm 91—all the promises, blessings, and a love letter from the Father to His children—and I are one.

Revelation 12:11 (NET) declares, "You have overcome the evil one by the blood of the Lamb and by the word of their [your] testimony."

This is the power of words. By speaking the Father's words, your faith grows, and you are building your confidence up by *only believing* what the Father has said. *God cannot lie.* This leads me to Psalm 91, one of my favorite books and scriptures in the Bible.

Wisdom runs with knowledge and understanding. Remember, when you find the word *you*, put your name there, and Psalm 91 becomes a love letter to you. Victory is through God's Word. He lives in you, His body. Faith to faith, partners in the journey. Have Bible, will travel.

★ PSALM 91 ★

I remember when I was reading Psalm 91 and saw the word *you* come up, I put my name there. Then the psalm became a love letter to me and the body of Christ. I said, "This is good." I felt like a little kid in a candy store. I read the psalm over and over. This is our (me and my family) protection, safety, and refuge.

Lucas, my grandson, was ten years old; and the dark was always scaring him. Fear would come. I said to Lucas, "Don't be afraid. God has promised protection." So we read Psalm 91, and I said to Lucas, "We will leave your Bible open all night."

When we (or you) read God's Word out loud, you are telling Satan that this is God's promise, and you are reminding the Father of His word for His children.

Do you remember when your mother and father took you to church, and you asked Jesus into your life? At that moment, all blessings and promises are yours, and you became joint heirs with Jesus as heirs of God. You are a citizen of the kingdom of God in heaven (the household of God).

The power of the Father's words created the earth in all its beauty for us. God is our hiding place, before time began.

Lucas has tasted the goodness of God and seen the Father's Word never come back void. So I study Psalm 91, and I am the Father's messenger—a watchman. The Word of God is for you, brothers and sisters. God is no respecter of persons. Please take the Word and eat the scroll. It is like honey.

Here is a love letter to His children, from the Father (Abba):

To all my children,

I am writing a love letter to all, all my children (kids), that you may keep with you forever and ever. My son Moses wrote a letter to me. It said, "Father, you have been my sanctuary since the beginning of time. Before the mountains were called into existence or born. Before you created the earth and the world, you were my Father God. You have always been and you will always be Yahweh, Father God."

I love this part of the letter because I love my son Moses. I love all my children the same. When I created my sons and daughters, I said I would take care of *you all* with my love and my words to comfort you. So I had Moses write a letter to every one of you, my children. You see, Father God does not have grown-ups in heaven—only children (kids). This love letter is a covenant, a promise strong and powerful. Words for my children (kids), simple and direct.

My sons and daughters who live and abide in the secret place (safe in my words) of the Most High shall dwell (live) under the shadow of the Almighty (Yahweh). I am your refuge (safety, protection, shielder) and fortress (shield of blood). In Me (Father), you can learn and rely on Me and trust Me. I will protect, save you from hidden traps and from deadly diseases. *I will* cover all of you with my feathers and under my wings. My truth, my Word, will be like armor and shield to all my children. Children, you will not be afraid of the danger by night or any accusations that fly by day, or of the diseases that walk in darkness or the sickness that strikes at high noon. A thousand will fall at your left side, ten thousand will fall at your right side, but *you will not be hurt*. Nor will it come near you.

Only with your eyes will you see the wicked get their reward and punishment. Because you, my sons and daughters, have made me (Father God) your refuge and safety, even the Most High your dwelling place. *No evil will come to destroy* or break you kids, nor shall any disaster come near *your dwelling* place (wherever you are). Your Father will give (ask, order, command) His angels charge to watch over all His children to keep you in all their ways (Hebrews 1:14).

The angels will bear you children up in their hands. You will not hit your foot on a rock. My children (kids) will walk (trample) on lions and snakes (demons). The young lions and dragon (Satan) you will trample, stamp, crush, flatten, destroy under your feet (Luke 10:19).

You kids have set your love upon Me, your Father. I will deliver *you all*, set *you all* on high, because *you all* know my name (Abba, Father, Yahweh). You will call upon Me (Father God), and I will answer you all. *I will* be with my children (kids) in trouble; *I will* deliver my kids and honor them all. Long life will I, Yahweh (Father), satisfy My children and show them My salvation (Genesis 6:3). Now eat *the scroll, the letter from the Father* (God).

This is a foundation to God's Word that you need to get in your spirit that will open all the Father's blessings and promises and His love letter. Numbers 23:19 (NET) says, "God is not a man *that He should lie*, nor a human being, that he should change his mind. He said, and will he not do it? Or He [God] spoken, and will He not make it happen [italics mine]."

In the International Children's Bible, it says, "God is not man. *He will not lie.* God is not a human being. *He does not change His mind.* What He says He will do, He does. What He promises, He keeps [italics mine]."

Titus 1:12 (NET) states, "In the hope of eternal, which God, *who does not lie,* promised before the age began [italics mine]."

Titus 1:2 (AMP) reads thus, "Base on the hope and divine guarantee of eternal life [the life] which God, *who is ever truthful and without deceit,* promised before the ages of time began [italics mine]."

Hebrews 6:17, 18 (ICB) states the following:

> God wanted to prove that His promise was true. He wanted to prove this to those who would get what He promised. He wanted them to understand clearly that His *purposes never change.* So God proved His promise by also making an oath. These two things *cannot change. God cannot lie* when He makes a promise, and *He cannot lie* when He makes an oath. These things encourage us who came to God for safety [Psalm 91]. They give us strength to hold on to the hope we have been given [italics mine].

Hebrews 6:17, 18 (Holman Christian Standard Bible) proclaims the following:

> Because God wanted to show His *unchangeable* purpose evermore clearly to the *heirs of promise,* He guaranteed it *with an oath,* so that through *two unchangeable things* in which it is impossible for God to lie, we who have *fled for refuge* [Psalm 91] might have strong encouragement to seize the hope set before us [italics mine].

We have *a foundation that cannot be moved.* As I have said before, God cannot lie. So with that note, let us go to Psalm 91. I will be using the New King James Version for my text:

1. He [us, we, you, I, Bryan] who dwells [live, reside, sanctuary] in the secret place [Psalm 119:114, 162] of the Most High shall [will, must] abide [live with, dwell, reside, sanctuary] under the shadow [protection, sanctuary] of the Almighty [Psalms 27:5, 31:20, 32:7, 17:8, 18:2].
2. I [Bryan] will say of the Lord [Jehovah], "He is my refuge [safety, shielder, protection, sanctuary] and my fortress [the blood of Christ, one-drop security, stronghold]; my God, in Him I will trust."
3. Surely [beyond doubt, without doubt, unquestionable] He [God] shall deliver you [me, my domain, my household] from the snare [traps] of the fowler [hunters of birds, fowl] and from the perilous [deadly] pestilence [diseases, (ICB) deadly diseases].
4. He [God] shall cover you [Bryan, me] with His feathers, and under His wings you [Bryan] shall take refuge [shelter, protection, safety, sanctuary]; His [God] truth shall be your [my, Bryan] shield [armor] and buckler [Psalm 17:8, Ephesians 6:10–17].
5. You [Bryan] shall not be afraid of the terror [fear, danger] by night nor the arrow [accusations] that flies by day.
6. Nor of pestilence [diseases] that walk in darkness, nor of the destruction [sickness] that lays waste at noonday [Isaiah 53:5, Matthew 8:17, 1 Peter 2:24].

7. A thousand may fall at your side and ten thousand at your [my] right hand; but it [danger, fear, sickness, diseases, accusations, disaster, sin, evil, whatever the world wants to throw at you] shall not come near you [Bryan, or hurt you, touch you].
8. Only with your [my] eyes shall you [Bryan] look and see the reward of the wicked.
9. Because you [Bryan] have made the Lord [Jehovah], who is my [Moses] refuge [safety, protection, shielder], even the Most High, your [my] habitation [dwelling place, residence, sanctuary].
10. No evil shall befall [come near, happen to, hurt] you [Bryan] nor shall any plague [disaster] come near your [my] dwelling [house, car, body] [Proverbs 12:21, 1 John 5:18, Luke 10:19];
11. For He [Father God] shall give [ask, order, command] His angels charge [watch] over you [Bryan, household, domain] to keep you [Bryan] in all your [my] ways [Hebrews 1:14].
12. They [angels] shall bear you [Bryan, me] up in their hands [palms] lest you [Bryan] dash your foot against a stone [Matthew 16:18, 19 (AMP)].
13. You [Bryan] shall tread [walk, trample] upon the lion and the cobra [adder, scorpion, snakes], the young lions and the serpent [dragon, demons] you [Bryan] shall trample [stomp, hurt, crush, flatten, destroy] underfoot [Luke 10:19, Revelation 12:11].
14. Because He [I, Bryan] has set his love upon me, Father God, therefore *I will* deliver him [Bryan, household, family]; *I will* set [exalt

him] him on high because he has known My name [Jehovah-Elohim, Jehovah-Elyon, El Shaddai, Jehovah-Jireh, Jehovah-Repheka, Jehovah-Tsidqenu, Jehovah-wissi, Jehovah-shalm, Jehovah-Shamah, Jehovah-Father, Jesus] [Psalm 9:10].
15. He [Bryan] shall call upon Me (Father God), and I *will answer him*; I (God, Father, Jesus) *will* be with him [me, Bryan] *in trouble*; *I will* deliver [set free, L. Berate] him [Bryan] and honor him [John 5:19 (present tense), John 14:14, John 15:7 (anything)].
16. With long life [length of days] *I will* satisfy him [Bryan] and show him My salvation [Jesus, my son] [Isaiah 54:17, Rec 12:11, Genesis 6:3 (120 years)] [italics mine].

Remember, in the beginning, *God does not lie*. Always remember this and *say* or *speak* God's words. Watch God work or his hands on the Word. When God's word leaves your mouth, you are giving birth to his word (speaking a miracle, healing, blessing). The word will never come back void, but the word will accomplish what the word was set out to do.

Proverbs 30:5 says, "Every word of God is pure." Psalm 12:6 states, "The Lord's words are absolutely reliable." Psalm 89:34, 35 (AMP) proclaims, "My covenant *I will not violate*, nor *will I alter the utterance of my lips* [italics mine]. Once (for all) I have sworn by my holiness, [my vow which cannot be violated; I will not lie to David]."

When God spoke the world and all that is in the earth, it was by his power of the word that everything came into existence. God's words are established in heaven and on the earth. The Father's words *will never be altered*. What He said, *He meant*.

Remember, *God cannot lie*. Now I would like to take you to Proverbs 4:20–22 (NKJV). "My son [Bryan], give [pay] attention to My [God's] words [listen to your Father's words]. Incline your ear to My saying [words]. Do not let them [my words] depart from your eyes; keep them [my words] in the midst [center] of your heart [spirit]; for they [my words] are life [treasure] to those who find them, and health [healing] to all their flesh [treasure hunt]."

A word though, unspoken, will die, unborn. God's Word, spoken, will give birth and/or life.

As I said before, *God cannot lie*. So let us go to Hebrews 1:3, which states, "Who being the brightness of His glory the *express image* of his person, and upholding all things *by the word of his power*, when he had by himself purged our sin, sat down at the right hand of the majesty on high."

The power of words—life or death, praise or condemnation, to edify or to tear down—that's what you have in your mouth. Look at Proverbs 6:2. It says, "You [Bryan] are snared [entangled] by the words of your mouth." Basically, what you say is what you get. Confession brings possession, and possession brings your words into reality. So you see, the power of words is very important in your walk with Christ.

Brother and sister, you have the *mind of Christ*; that's in God's Word (1 Corinthians 2:16 (mind), 2 Corinthians 4:4 (image), 2 Corinthians 11:33 (not living), 1 Peter 1:13). In order to cultivate (develop, improve, nourish, discipline) it, you must read God's Word daily. Don't throw your Bible in the back seat of your car or truck for next Sunday but open God's Word and see *who you are, what you have*, and *what you can do* in the Father's words.

Some say there are three thousand promises in the Bible, blessings and promises that belong to the children of God. Remember, you are born into God's family, joint heirs with Christ. Romans 8:17 states, "Now if we are children, then we are heirs—heirs of God and co-heirs with Christ, if indeed we share in His sufferings in order that we may also share in His glory."

Here are some more scriptures: 1 Peter 1:4; John 1:12; Matthew 25:24; Galatians 3:29; and Colossians 1:12, 3:24. You can look the scriptures up for yourself. Out of your truck or out of your car and to the kitchen table.

Now I like doing puzzles, so God gave me my first piece. Hebrews 4:12 (WKJU) says, "For the word of God is living [active, anointed, working, quick-swift] and powerful [effective, authority, in control, omnipotent] and sharper than any two-edged sword, piercing even to the division of soul and spirit, and joints and marrow, and is a discerner [the dictionary says "to perceive by sight or some other sense or by the intellect"; see *recognize* or *apprehend*) of the thoughts and intents of the heart (a treasure hunt)."

My first piece. I was like a little kid in the candy store. When I was eight years old, every Saturday, I would go to the corner store (Glen Party Store in Westland, Michigan) with a dime and would come home with twenty pieces of candy, two for a penny. *Do you remember?* Then the Father said to me, "My word is established in heaven and on the earth. My word will never change. I meant what I said. I am your Father, Bryan." God *cannot lie* or *does not lie*. Lying is not in heaven.

That is why you must speak His word and hold to the Father's words and remind him of what he said. The Father likes that.

There are prayers in the Bible you need to read daily. There is a book called *In Him* by Kenneth E. Hagin. You need it in your library. Ephesians 1:15–33, Ephesians 3:14–21, and Colossians 1:9–14 are three of the eight prayers that I prayed; and they changed my view, or outlook, of God's Word.

This is the power of words. Now listen to the Father's Word. In Ephesians 4:29, it says, "Let no corrupt communication proceed out of your mouth, but what is good for necessary edification [building up], that it may impart grace to the hearer." As I was cross-referencing Ephesians 4:29 with the Amplified Bible, this is what it said, and I like it. Ephesians 4:29 (AMP) states, "Do not let unwholesome [foul, profane, worthless, vulgar] words ever come out of your mouth, but only such speech as is good for building up others, according to the need and the occasion, so that it will be a blessing to those who hear [you speak]." So when you speak to individuals wherever you are at, *only speak God's words, for they give life.*

How powerful are the Father's words? You are armed with the truth of God's Word. You have the armor of God on you if you read His Word. Take the Bible off the shelf and dust it off. Now go to Ephesians 6:13–17. It reads as follows:

> Therefore take up the whole armor of God, that you [Bryan] may be able to withstand in the evil day, and having done all to stand [in the gap], stand therefore, having girded [to prepare oneself for action] your waist with truth, having put on the breastplate of righteousness [uprightness; *moral essence*, his way of doing and being right, the attitude and character of God] [Genesis 15:6, Matthew 5:20, Matthew 6:33 (AMP)], and having shod your feet with the preparation of the gospel of peace; *above all*, taking the shield of faith with which you [Bryan] will be able to quench all the fiery darts of the wicked one. And take the helmet of salvation, and the sword of the spirit, which is the word of God.

This is the power of God's word, which I have written down. The full armor of God you must have daily, so read God's Word and learn what power you have in Christ, joint heirs of Jesus. Look at Hebrews 6:5, which states, "And have tasted the good word of God and the power of the age to come." The ICB translation is very good; I like it. It states, "They found out how good God's word is, and they received the power of his new world." The power of God's Word can and will pull down strongholds. The Father said to the body, "I have given you authority and power in my words. Do not let them fall by the side of the of the road or in the back seat of your car. *Remember* the sower of the seeds in Matthew (Matthew 13:1–8)."

Revelation 12:11 says, "They [us, I, you] overcame him [Satan] by the blood of the Lamb and by word of their [us, I, you] testimony."

I have learned who I am in Christ, and that is my testimony, for Jesus has delivered me from the power of darkness and transferred me into the kingdom of the son of his love (Colossians 1:13–14) *in whom* I have redemption through His blood (the forgiveness of sins).

I have said only what the word of the Father has said in the Bible. Father's words are my testimony. I have his nature in me, his DNA. All that God is lives in me.

I know who I am, I know what I have, and I know what I can do. I know who has my back—that is Jesus, my big brother. And my father has the back of Jesus.

Matthew 28:18 (NKJV) says, "Then Jesus came and spoke to them [disciples], saying 'All [complete, full, entire, greatest] authority [power] has been given to me [Jesus Christ] in Heaven and Earth.'" So the power is given to the body, the church of believers.

With this in mind, I would like to give you more scriptures. Proverbs 3:23–27 (AMP) states the following:

> Then you will walk on your way [of life] securely, and your foot will not stumble. When you lie down, you will not be afraid. When you lie down, your sleep will be sweet. Do not be afraid, sudden fear nor of the storm of the wicked when it comes [since you will be blameless]; for the Lord will be your confidence, firm and strong, and will keep your foot from being caught [entrapped]. Do not withhold good from those to whom it is due [its rightful recipients], when it is in your power to do it.

Proverbs 1:33 (AMP) says, "But whoever listens to me (Wisdom) will live securely and in confident trust and will be at ease, without fear or dread of evil."

God's promises for protection are in Psalm 91. You can and should look up in your Bible all of these scriptures:

> Behold, I am with you and will keep you wherever you go. (Genesis 28:15 ASV)

> I will both lie down in peace and sleep; for you alone, O Lord, made me dwell in safety. (Psalm 4:8)

> Whoever listens to me will dwell safely, and will be secure, without fear of evil. (Proverbs 1:33)

The Lord is my light and my salvation; whom shall I fear? The Lord is the strength of my life; of whom shall I be afraid? (Psalm 24:1)

The beloved of the Lord shall dwell in safety by Him, who shelters Him all the day long. (Deuteronomy 33:12)

He shall give His angels charge over you, to keep you in all your ways. (Psalm 91:11)

I will say of the Lord, "He is my refuge and my fortress; my God in Him I will trust." (Psalm 91:2)

The name of the Lord is a strong tower; the righteous run to it and are safe. (Proverbs 18:10)

For I know whom I have believed and am persuaded that he is able to keep what I have committed to Him until that day. (2 Timothy 1:12)

Though I walk in the midst of trouble, you will revive me; you will stretch out your hand against the wrath of my enemies, and your right hand will save me. (Psalm 138:7)

I will put you in the cleft of the rock and will cover you with my hand. (Exodus 33:22)

He who dwells in the secret place of the Most High shall abide under the shadow of the Almighty. (Psalm 91:1)

Who is he who will harm you if you become followers of what is good? (1 Peter 3:13)

> As the mountains surround Jerusalem, so the Lord surrounds his people from this time forth and forever. (Psalm 125:2)

> The angel of the Lord encamps all around those who fear Him, and delivers them. (Psalm 34:7)

> Many are the afflictions of the righteous, but the Lord delivers him out of them all. (Psalm 34:19)

The joy of the Lord and His promises and blessing are yours from the Father. This is the power of God's Word that has been spoken to the body of Christ. Amen.

I like what the centurion said in Luke 7:1–10 and Matthew 8:5–13. The centurion in Luke said, "Just *say* the word, and my servant we be healed." In Matthew, the centurion said, "*Speak* the word, and my servant will be healed." The centurion was saying, "I don't have to see. I know." He recognized the authority Jesus has. For he heard what my Lord did for other people. That same authority is ours, for we are the body of Christ.

John 16:14, 15 (AMP) tells us, "He [Holy Spirit] will glorify and honor me, because he [Holy Spirit] will take from *what is mine* and *will disclose* [declare, tell it] to you [italics mine]."

In 1 Corinthians 3:21–23, it says, "So let no one boast in men [about their wisdom of having this or that one as a leader]. For all things are yours, whether Paul or Apollos or Cephas [Peter] or the world or life or death or things present or things to come; *all things are yours*, and you belong to Christ, and Christ belongs to God [Jehovah]."

This is the covenant that Jesus Christ made. Everything God has belongs to us (the body). The Father gave it to Jesus, and He gave it to us. *All the things are ours* (yours, mine). We are surrounded by the power of God and His words that live in us. Christ lives in you, for you are the temple of the living God. *All things are yours*, joint heirs with Christ. That is why I can say or speak God's Word with authority, because God backs up his words.

The Father cannot lie. Get it in your spirit today by reading Jehovah's (the Father's) Word, and speak His Word and believe what you say. You have it.

Mark 11:23, 24 (NET) reads as follows:

> I tell you the truth, if someone says to this mountain; be lifted up and thrown into the sea, and does not doubt in his heart [in God's unlimited power] but believes that what he says will happen, it will be done for him [in accordance with God's will]. For this reason I tell you, whatever you pray and ask for, believe [with confident trust] that you have received it [your prayers], and they will be yours.

My dad (J. D. Hines) and my two brothers (Paul and Mike) went salmon fishing in Lake Michigan. But on that day, it was raining, and the water on the lake was bad. It was so bad, the two boats were trying to get to the cove for safety.

As I watched, both boats were lying on their sides; so I asked the Lord to bring them home in one piece, which God did. Then the Father reminded me of the Sea of Galilee.

That day, Jesus was sleeping, and his disciples said, "Lord, we are perishing." So Jesus got up from His sleep and rebuked the wind. The disciples said, "What authority this man has. Even the wind obeys him." And so I said, "I came two thousand and five hundred miles to go fishing, and we have bad weather." I remembered God's words. I said "be still" to the wind, and the water was like glass. I walked away, and the wind stopped and the lake was like glass. (I don't have to see. I know.)

We did not catch salmon, so I asked the Lord, "Why no fish?" And he made me laugh. The Father said, "You did not ask, Bryan. Only that the weather had to change. You see, I was there hoping for you to believe, as you ask me to do things for you." Only believe.

I remember the time I transplanted a black walnut tree in my backyard. I asked my grandson Lucas to cut the backyard. He was fourteen at the time. As he was cutting the yard, Lucas cut down my black walnut tree. He thought it was a weed. I said to him, "That is okay. We will agree to Matthew 18:19." (You look it up.) So I said, "Lord, bring back the tree strong and heathy in Jesus's name."

Two weeks later, the tree was six inches tall (remember he cut the tree to the ground), so I put an edge, or border, around the tree. I showed the tree to Lucas, how our prayer was answered. Lucas cut the backyard again, and he cut the tree down again. When he told me, I was mad. I yelled at him so bad that he cried. *I wounded his spirit.*

The Lord said, "Apologize now." I did and we agreed God would raise the dead tree again. This time, the tree was nine inches tall in two weeks. Lucas came and saw what Jesus did to answer our prayers.

Now the story is going to get really good. Lucas cut the tree down again a third time. I was sitting in my chair when I was told the tree was cut down. I looked at him and said, "That's okay, buddy. Don't worry about it. It's only a tree."

So I kept on watching the TV. Then the Father said, "Aren't you going to pray and ask me to heal the tree?"

I said, "No. I am mad, and I don't care if the tree dies."

So two weeks later, the tree was twelve inches tall. I called for Lucas to come and see the black walnut tree. Lucas said to me, his grandfather, "I know. I prayed over the tree."

Out of the mouths of babes comes wisdom.

I learned two things that day. Everything I tell my grandkids, they listen (remember). And God is no respecter of persons. Oh, and one more thing. God humbled me that day to another level.

My third story is about my fishing bobber. Lucas and I went to Old Hickory Lake in Tennessee, but I only had little bobbers. I forgot the medium-sized ones. As we were fishing, my bobber came off. Now I know how to connect a bobber to the line. I have been fishing all my life. I asked the Father to bring my bobber back to me. We were fishing off the shore, and the bobber was two feet away. I said, "Lord, you bring me the bobber closer, and I will get the bobber." But the bobber was floating away. "Father, what do you want?"

The Lord said, "Ask me for another bobber."

"Father, my bobber is not far from me. Just push it to me."

Then God said, "Ask for a bobber, my son."

So I said, "Okay. I need a medium-size bobber, and it should be brand-new."

As Lucas and I were fishing, my open face spinning reel lashed back (the lines went backward) on me. After, I told Lucas about the bobber that I asked God for. I said to Lucas, "Go get your tackle box and fishing gear, and let us go sit at the round table so I can fix my reel."

Lucas and I turned our heads at the same time, and there, under an oak tree, was the new medium-sized bobber that I asked for. Then the Father said, "I want to take care of the small things, just as I take care of you and your family."

Three stories, the *power of words*, and Psalm 91. When God says or speaks His word, what proceeds out of God's mouth, His lips, He will not alter. I go back to Psalm 91. I live in the sanctuary of God's word, for that is how I know my Father's will for my life and my family. I am royalty. I am a prince in my Father's kingdom. I am a watchman, one who cries in the wilderness, "Repent for the kingdom of God is at hand. Salvation is today." I am a prophet with words of encouragement, edification, uplifting with God's words. I am an apostle of God, a saint—all that the Father said I am.

So are you, brothers and sisters. So are you. Remember, God is no respecter of persons. What the Father did for Mark, John, Peter, Timothy, and his children in the Old Testament, He will do for you.

The Father never lied to David, and David was the apple of God's eye! *God will not lie to you.* The devil is the father of *all lies*. So when you read Psalm 91 out loud, you are reminding the devil what the Father has spoken, and you are reminding the Father of His words. God likes that. That's one way His words are getting inside of you (your spirit).

Remember Lucas and the black walnut tree. Kids, or children, hear everything you say and remember everything you do. They will *imitate* their parents when you read the Word of God. Jesus *imitated* His Father. Christ spoke only what the Father spoke and only what the Father showed Him. Jesus *imitated* his Father, and we need to *imitate* Christ, our brother, the firstborn of the Father. Brothers and sisters in the family of God, we are citizens of heaven.

Psalm 119:11 reads, "Your word I have treasured and stored in my heart, that I may not sin against you."

Psalm 119:11 (New American Bible, Revised Edition) states, "In my heart I treasure your *promise*, that I may not sin against you [italics mine]."

The promises and blessings that are in the Bible are ours. If you do not hide God's Word, you cannot stand against the enemy that will attack you daily. I have talked to many people about Psalm 91, and I believe all the blessings and promises in the Bible are in Psalm 91.

Let us go to Ephesians 1:15–23. The beginning of the church (authority), a prayer of revelation that Paul wrote to the saints in Ephesians, that is you. When I come to the word *you*, I put my name there so the letter is personal (a love letter).

In the New King James Version, it is stated as follows:

> Therefore I [Paul] do not cease to give thanks for you [Bryan], making mention of you [Bryan] in my prayer; that the God of our Lord Jesus Christ, the Father of glory, may give to you [Bryan] the spirit of wisdom and revelation in the knowledge of Him [Father] the eyes of your [Bryan] understanding being enlightened; that you [Bryan] may know what is the hope of His calling, what are the riches of the glory of His inheritance in the saints, and what is the exceeding greatness of His power towards us [Bryan] who believe, according to the working of his mighty power which He [Father] worked in Christ when He raised Him [Christ] from the dead and seated Him [Christ] at His right hand in the heavenly places [overcome] *far above all* principality [rule] and power [authority] and might [power] and dominion, and every name

> that is named, not only in this age but also in that which is to come, and He [Father] *put all things* [everything] under His [Jesus] feet, and gave Him [Christ] to be head over *all things* to the church, which is His body, the fullness of Him [Father God] who fills in all. (See Matthew 28:18 on authority.)

Now this prayer changed my life forever, for Paul prayed for me to have wisdom and revelation of the knowledge of Him (Father, Jesus).

I went back to God's Word with that wisdom and knowledge and asked for an *illumination* of His word and life. It was like turning the bright light on, you can imagine. I see the presence of God in His Word. I see His nature. I see what He put on the table (Psalm 23:5) before my enemies is *everything* you need in the world, and here are just a few of the spiritual foods. Grace, mercy, love, peace, joy, the goodness of God, patience, courage, boldness, confidence, salvation, righteousness, deliverance, fulfillment, authority, strength, shelter, safety, protection, security, discipline, truth, sanctuary—these are only a few. There are a lot more. Whatever you need is on the table. Remember this when you are standing before your enemies.

This is the *power of God's Word.* "Only believe" is what Smith Wigglesworth would always say. I will say the same words, "Only believe." Remember Luke 7:1–10 or Matthew 8:5–10. Just speak the word or say the word. This is what Jesus is saying to His body, "I have spoken God's word to you, and you do not believe. Oh, you of little faith." This is why you must read the Father's Word (letters). He does not lie!

I have eaten from my table many times. I keep going back when I am hungry for more of God—for the wisdom, knowledge, understanding, and authority that has been given to me and to you. Go back to Ephesians 2:1, 6, which reads, "And you [Bryan] He [God] made alive, who were dead in trespasses and sins, and raised us [body] up together, and made us [body] sit together in the heavenly places in Christ Jesus." You are born again and are sitting with Jesus in heaven.

The Power of God's Word

Colossians 3:13 states, "You [Bryan] have been set free from Satan." Jesus has delivered us (the body, Bryan) from the power of darkness and transferred us (the body, Bryan) into the kingdom of the Son of His love, *in whom* we (the body) have redemption (deliverance from sin, salvation) through His blood, the forgiveness of sin. There is a saying that proclaims, "You have been set free." You are free indeed. When Jesus said, "It is finished," it was His part of the journey. And the second he said it, the body (believers) became the light in the world. We are His, and He is ours.

Philippians 2:9, 10 reads as follows:

> God equipped us [body] with authority and power through His name [Jesus]. Therefore, God [Father] also has highly exalted Him [Christ] and given Him [Christ] the name of Jesus every knee should bow, of those in heaven, and of those on earth, and of those under the earth, and that every tongue should confess that Jesus Christ is Lord, to the glory of God the Father.

When you say the name of Jesus, you have the attention of all the angels and demons in hell waiting for your orders or commands, not to mention the weather and everything around you. There is power in God's word "Jesus." This is my story on Lake Michigan. I call on Jesus's name because I am joint heir with Him. I am sitting in heaven with Him. Where I go, Jesus goes. My buddy.

I remember a doll "my buddy of boys many years ago. I will try to remember the song: "My Buddy, my buddy wherever I go, he goes. My buddy, my buddy, he teaches me everything he knows. My buddy and me are great friends, you see." Christ is more than a brother. He is my friend. Jesus calls me friend.

He walks with me and talks to me every day of my life. All that I am saying to my brothers and sisters in the Lord is, without reading the Bible, God's Word, you would not know who you are, what you have, and what you can do in the name of Jesus. How many promises and blessings are yours? All that God (Father) has (John 16:13–15) belongs to us, his body.

In Genesis 1:3, God said, "Let us make man *in our image, according to our likeness*, let them [man] have dominion over the fish of the sea, over the birds of the air, and over the cattle, *over all the earth* and over every creeping thing that creeps on the earth [italics mine]."

Ephesians 4:24 (NET) says, "Put on the new man who has been created in God's image and likeness—righteousness and holiness that comes from truth."

Ephesians 4:24 reads, "And put on the new self [the regenerated and renewed nature] *created in God's likeness*, our likeness, God the Father, God the Son, God the Holy Spirit, the three spirits of God. In the beginning of time [italics mine]."

Now let's go to the New Testament and see what Jesus said about himself:

> I tell you the solemn truth, the Son can do nothing on his own initiative, but only what he sees the Father doing. For whatever the Father does, the Son does likewise. For the Father loves the Son and *shows him everything he does*, and will show him greater deeds than these, so that you will be amazed [italics mine]. (John 5:19, 20 NET)

> For the bread of God is the one who comes down from heaven and gives life to the world. Then Jesus declared, "I am the bread of life. The one who comes to me will never go hungry, and the one who believes in me will never be thirsty." (John 6:33, 35 NET)

These are only a few scriptures I gave to you; there are more in God's Word. Read the holy scriptures today and see Jehovah's promise and blessing and His love letter to you. Ask and receive. Knock and the door will open. Seek the Father, and I tell you, you will find Him.

When I was sixteen, I started using a metal detector to look for coins people lose—coin shooting. Then as I got older, I was a coach hunter (looking for big treasure). I had to read and learn all about treasure hunting as a business: the law of each state, US government laws, and IRS laws. So I also talked to older treasure hunters for wisdom. You could say I picked their brains or mined them for information. I seek God's nature through His words, to know Him.

So this is what I found in His word of Father God: sanctuary, shelter, safety, protection, security, stronghold, shield of the blood of Christ, mercy, grace, my love, righteousness, joy, peace, my DNA, nature, Father, Lord, King, armor, habitation, reside, abide, live with, shield, shadow of the Almighty, true, trust, beyond doubt, deliver, feather, honor, dwelling place, set me on high, long life, I am satisfied, my salvation, I shall not want, shepherd, green pastures, water, restores, my soul, rod and staff, comfort, anointing oil, my cup, goodness, everlasting to everlasting, wisdom, knowledge, glory, understanding, healing, mirror, gift, strength, fullness of Him, treasure, complete in Him, power, two-edged sword, mountain dissolver, word, compassion, gracious, abounding in goodness and truth, workmanship, blessing, holy place, gladness, excellent, pure, likeness, perfect, rock, gentleness, and deliverer.

As I read my Bible, I see my Father in every word on every page. I seek my Father out. Seek and you will find. I am a treasure hunter, and I found a great treasure in a mountain (my front yard), and I sold all I had and bought the mountain to have the greatest treasure ever found.

I was twenty-five in my front yard in Irving, Texas, when that treasure (or gift) was found, and I have not been the same.

God does not lie. "In Christ are hidden all the treasures of wisdom and knowledge" (Colossians 2:3). Find the treasure in Christ today for tomorrow and forever. Amen!

I would like to quote three wise men I have read, and I know one personally.

Dr. John Lake wrote, "I believe the law of the spirit of life in Christ Jesus has set me free from the law of sin and death. As long as I walk in the light of that life, no germ will attach itself to me." Amen!

Smith Wigglesworth, the great English apostle of faith, said, "I am not moved by what I feel. I am not move by what I see. I am moved only by what I believe. I cannot understand God by feelings. I understand God by what the Word says about Him. I understand the Lord Jesus Christ by what the word says about Him. He is everything the Word says that He is."

B. D. Featherchicken also says, "I am not moved by what I see. I am not moved by what I hear. I am not moved by what I feel. I am moved only by the Word of God. That's the truth."

The truth is in the Word of God. What the Father says is who He is. So I go back to Psalm 91, to what the Father has said. Everything is ours, the believers. I have learned to use what skills I have been taught in my treasure-hunting days: to read and take notes. But I like the Holy Spirit (of God) the most, for He teaches me the mysteries and the secrets in the Father's Word.

Freely as you have received, give it away. Do not keep it (God's word) to yourself. The Father's word is to edify and build up the spirit of the person (the body). You have the authority to use His name (Jesus) to speak life to the world. Call for healing and miracles all around you. Do not let Satan steal from you what you have. Confess God's word in your life and *others*. You have everything you ever need to live in the world. Jesus said, "I overcame the world." And so have you.

The Father is faithful to His words. The Father does not change, does not waver. He spoke it (everything) into existence and gave birth to what He said.

Hebrews 10:23 (AMP) says, "Let us seize and hold tightly the confession of our hope without wavering, for He [the Father] who promised is reliable and trustworthy and faithful [to His word]."

Now this is the new covenant God (Father) made with the House of Israel and Judah:

> "For this is the covenant that *I will* make with the house of Israel after those days," said the Lord. "*I will* imprint [write, inscribe my laws; Father's word] upon their minds [even upon their innermost thoughts and understanding] and engrave [tattoo] them upon their hearts [their spirit, effecting their regeneration], and *I will* be their God [Father], and they shall be my people."

The Father made a covenant, a promise, and a love letter to His children (you and me). God is faithful to His words. He is never late and is always on time. That is why we have Psalm 91 to remind us of that promise from the beginning of time. "*I* (the Father) *will* take care of everything, and you shall not want."

Psalm 23:1 (AMP) proclaims, "The Lord is my shepherd [to feed, to guide, and to shield me]. I shall not want [lack nothing]." I have all I need according to God's Word, faithful and true. My dad (JD) would say, "You can tell if a man is honest to his word with a handshake. And if he keeps what he says is true, his word will come to pass."

Everything the Father said will and has come to pass, and there is more to come. Amen. God never leaves you or forsakes you. He walks with you daily.

I was reading Genesis and how God would walk with Adam in the cool of the morning. I asked God to walk with me like He did with Adam, to walk by my side. I was taking groceries out to a customer's car, and on my way back to the store, I stopped. The Father said, "I am here all day, my son, by your side." I knew without a doubt my Father was with me.

We talked off and on through the day. When I was off my shift, I thanked my Father. God said, "*I will* never leave you or forsake you. When you are in trouble, *I am* there. You have angels to walk with you. I love you, Bryan."

I cried that day. When I talk about my experience with my Father, I cry. I want the body to have that experience, and the Father wants you to have the same. *Seek* God out, and you will find him.

Knock and the door will open. Ask and you will get your heart's desire.

I did and I will never be the same again. I have tasted the goodness of God, and I want more, and there is more. It is the *greatest treasure* I have ever found in all my years of hunting treasure in my front yard in Irving, Texas, at 4:30 am. The thing that is amazing about this treasure is that it keeps growing, and there is no end in sight.

Brothers and sisters, treasure hunters, you found the greatest treasure of all (Jesus) in your front yard. And the treasure just keeps growing daily.

Read the Father's Word and grab hold of Psalm 91. It is yours—a covenant, a promise, a love letter from Yahweh (your Father).

For all my King James Version, here is the Dake Bible version of Psalm 91:

> He that [individuals] dwelleth [Heb. *yashab*] [set down, dwell, settle, homestead] in the secret [Heb. *sether*] [covering, God's word, hiding place] place of the most High *shall abide* under the [secret place of the Most High, protection] shadow of the Almighty [God all-powerful]. I will say of the Lord, He is my refuge and my fortress [hiding place, fortress, protection, place of security]. My God; *in Him will I trust* [place of safety, protection, trust]. Surely [deliver you from hunters, trappers, deadly diseases, cover you with His wings] he shall deliver you from the snare [wicked man, fallen angels, and demons] of the fowler, and from the noisome [has-hauuah] [rushing calamity, deadly diseases] pestilence. *He* [God] *shall* cover you [Bryan] with his feathers [protection and care], and under his [God's] wings shalt thou [you] trust: [flee to refuge] his [God] truth shall be your shield [armor] and buckler [shield, protection of body from weapons and arrows], thou shalt not [you will not

The Power of God's Word

fear any danger by night] be afraid for the terror [treasons, plunderers, robbers, murderers, evils, and diseases] by night; nor [or] for the arrows [accusation] that flieth by day; nor [or] for pestilence [diseases at night] that walk in darkness; nor [or] for the destruction [sickness] that wasteth [strikes, ravages] at noonday. A thousand *shall fall* at your side, and ten thousand at your right hand, *but it shall not* [you will not be hurt] come nigh thee. Only with your eyes *shall thou* [you] behold and see the reward of the wicked [punished] *because* [secret place, refuge, fortress, God is your God, trust, deliverer, protection, shield, be not afraid, confidence, refuge, habitation, love, authority, call on God in prayer] thou [you] has made the Lord, which is my [Moses] refuge, even the most High, thy [your] habitation [dwelling place]; *there shall no evil* [Dake 1047] [all of Psalm 91; many are the promises of God, they cover every known need of life] befall thee [you] neither shall any plague [disaster will come to your home] come nigh thy [your] dwelling [home, body, temple]. *For He* [God] *shall* give His angels charge [orders, command, watch] over thee [you] *to keep* [protect] thee [you] in all thy [your] ways. They [angels] *shall* bear thee [you] up in their hands, *lest* thou [you] dash thy [your] foot against a stone. Thou shalt [you will] [promises power over all animals, insects, Satan, demons] tread [walk, trample] upon the lion and adder [snakes]; The young lion and the dragon [demons] shalt thou [you will] trample [step, hurt, stomp, destroy, crush, flatten] under feet. *Because* he hath set his love upon me [Father], therefore *will I* deliver him: *I will* set him on high, because he hath known my name: He shall call upon Me [God], and I will answer him: *I will* be with him [you] in trouble; *I will* deliver him and honour him. With long life *will I* satisfy him, and shew him [you] my salvation [italics mine].

We are partners in the journey—faith to faith, iron sharpens iron. Have Bible, will travel. Pray, warriors and soldiers of God's (Father's) army. You are more than a warrior. You are royalty. You are His (God's) sons and daughters, joint heirs with Christ and heirs of God (Father). You have everything!

Remember, God does not lie!

Amos 3:3 (ICB) reads, "Two people will not walk together unless they have agreed to do this."

Agree with the Father at all costs. Never turn your back or say *no*. (I have and it was not good. The Father disciplined me because He loves me so much.)

Your brother in Christ,

Evangelist B. D. Featherchicken

It is finished.

—A quote from Jesus, my Lord

PS: *What did he finish?* The work that the Father sent Him to do. *What was that work* that Jesus, the firstborn, set out to do for the Father? For that answer, we must look to the Father's Word.

Jesus came into the world to reconcile the human race back to the Father. For sin separated (not joined or touching) us from God (Father). Jesus, the firstborn of many brothers and sisters, had to die for us sinners so we too could have fellowship with the Father (Abba). This is it in a nutshell, but we treasure hunters must read the clues and the signs to get to the greatest treasure ever (Christ).

John 3:16 (NET) states, "For this is the way God [Father] loved the world: He gave His one and only Son, so that everyone who believes in Him [Jesus] will not perish, but have eternal life."

John 3:16 (AMP) reads, "For God so [greatly] loved and dearly prized the world, that he [even] gave His [one and] only begotten Son, so that whoever believes and trusts in Him [as Savior] shall not perish, but have eternal life."

This is the beginning of our hunt to find the *what* in his ministry.

Galatians 3:13, 14 (AMP) says, "Christ purchased our freedom and redeeming us from the cure [doom] of the law and its condemnation by [himself] becoming a curse for us, for it is written [in the scriptures] cursed is everyone who hangs [crucified] on a tree [cross]."

Deuteronomy 21:23 proclaims to the end that through [their receiving] Christ Jesus, the blessing [promised] to Abraham might come upon the gentiles, so that we through faith might all receive [the realization of] the promise of the [Holy] Spirit through faith.

Jesus manifested in the flesh was supernatural, and He became the Son of Man. Our new birth is supernature from God, born of spirit as well as the flesh. Jesus was given power to lay his life down and pick his life up. He, Jesus, is the Lamb for the world. "I am the way, the truth, and the life. And no one can come to the Father but by me."

Jesus is the Son of God, for God said in John 3:16, "This is my beloved Son in whom I am well pleased." God gave us the Holy Ghost to do the work of Jesus here on earth now. Jesus is the *author* of life here on earth, and He is alive. *We are His witness here on earth.*

Going to heaven, Jesus took the same way He came. Jesus is coming back soon. *He died once* for this world. The Holy Ghost was sent here to *finish* the work of Jesus, and *we are to finish his works.* The Holy Ghost will lead you and equip you here on earth. Jesus is coming back for a church, a bride with no spots or blemishes. *Are you listening to me!* He (Jesus) took the sting out of death when He died on the cross. He took the key of hell when He came out of the grave. Jesus set me (us) free. Jesus disarmed principalities and powers and put them to open shame. He overcame the world, and so have I.

When Jesus died on the cross, He did so much for the human race that day. We only have to touch the hem of His garment. We need to stand up and hold His hand and walk in His image on earth. Are you washed in His blood? Are you made whole? You are. You can do everything Jesus did today. What did He finish on the cross? You will never know as long as you keep your Bible in the car or on a shelf in the house.

You have to read God's Word to know (1) who you are, (2) what you have, and (3) what you can do. Most of the Christians are not serious about their walk with Christ. You have power that is given to you though His name (Jesus) and His blood and your testimony of who you are (Revelation 12:11).

We are the Father's sons and daughters, joint heirs of Jesus and heirs of God, my Father. Jesus gave us His body, the authority and power to walk this world (Luke 10:19). Psalm 91 says that God's angels are watching over you.

Get born again and washed in the blood of the Lamb. Only one drop of His blood (Christ) will make you clean today. Your name is written in the Lamb's Book of Life. We will rule with Him on earth together for a thousand years. When Jesus died, He opened the storehouse of blessings and promises from the Father for us, His children.

It is finished. His death set us free. His death gave us authority. His death has washed us with His blood. His death is the completion of the Father's work. His death gave us the Holy Ghost. His death gave us God's Word that is established in heaven and on earth. His death gave us healing. His death broke the curse. His death put God's word into action (Hebrews 4:12). In His death, I am more than a conqueror. I have won. In His death, He gave me a new life. Only I can touch the hem of the garment. His death gave me His mind. His death allowed Him to stand at the door and knock. His death gave me wisdom, knowledge, and understanding. With His death, it is finished. With His death, I shall not want (Psalm 23). His death set a table before all my enemies. His death gave me blessing, promise, and a love letter from the Father. His death gave me the right to go to the Father. His death gave me the right to go to the Father face-to-face. His death gave me all authority and power on earth.

As I was writing, I was thinking of all the brothers in the Old Testament that wrote by the inspiration of God and the New Testament writers, the revelation of which they received from God to write the Bible (Hebrews 10:7).

It's all about Jesus, the Son of Man—the Son of God doing the Father's will. It is finished. But it is never finished with me, for Jesus teaches me every single day. He is my treasure that grows and grows.

You must read the Bible to see how the greatest treasure grows. Then you have to; you must give it away! No matter what the cost is.

I leave you with 1 Corinthians 15:20 (AMP), which states, "But now [as things really are] Christ has in fact been raised from the dead, [and he became] the first fruits [that is, the first to be resurrected with an incorruptible, immortal body, foreshadowing the resurrection] of those who have fallen asleep [in death]."

PPS:

> "For I, the Lord, will speak whatever word I speak will be accomplished. It will not be delayed any

longer. Indeed in your day, O rebellious house, I will speak the word and accomplish it," declares the sovereign Lord. (Ezekiel 12:25 NET)

"For I, the Lord, will speak, and whatever word I speak will be accomplished. It will no longer be delayed, for in your days, O rebellious house, I will speak the word and I will fulfill it," says the Lord God [Father]. (Ezekiel 12:25 AMP)

Treasures beyond your imagination—that is what's in God's Word and His power!

Oh, Lord God, you did indeed make heaven and earth by your mighty power and great strength. *Nothing is too hard for you!* [italics mine] (Jeremiah 32:17 NET)

DO YOU REMEMBER?

Do you not remember, or do you not know, that the spirit of God lives in you?

Do you not remember, or do you not know, that Christ lives in you?

Do you not remember, or do you not know, that the Holy Spirit lives in you?

Do you not remember, or do you not know, that you live in the Father, the Son Jesus, and the Holy Spirit?

Do you not remember you are in the household of God, or do you not know (Ephesians 2:19–21)?

Do you not remember that no harm can come against you, or do you not know (Psalm 91:7)?

Do you not remember that you are His workmanship, or do you not know (Ephesians 2:10)?

Do you not remember you were made in the image and according to the likeness of God, or do you not know (Genesis 1:26)?

Do you not remember what was on the table God made before your enemies (must read the Father's Word), or do you not know (Psalm 23:5)?

Do you not remember that you have been anointed with power and authority from the Father, or do you not know?

Do you not remember you have the mind of Christ in you, or do you not know?

You have Jesus in you and his mind, and also kingdom thinking—retraining to think, walk, and speak like Him. That's the example we (His body) have to live by. Christ did everything the Father said to Him. He was obedient until death. Jesus walked humbly with the Father.

THE MIND OF CHRIST

Isa. 26:3 Perfect peace, whose mind (God's mind in us—trusts)
Mark 5:15 Clothed and in his right mind
Luke 12:29 (AMP) Doubtful mind
Acts 17:11 Received the word—readiness of mind
Acts 20:19 Served with humility of mind
Rom. 8:7 Carnal mind is enmity against God
Rom. 8:27 The spirit knoweth what is the mind of Christ
Rom. 11:34 Know the mind of the Father
Rom. 12:6 Same mind toward one another
Rom. 12:16 Mind not high things, but condescend
Rom. 14:5 Fully persuaded in His own mind
Rom. 15:6 With one mind, glorify God
1 Cor. 2:16 We have the mind of Christ (key)
2 Cor. 8:12 Willing mind
Phil. 2:3 Like mind—same love—one accord—one mind
Phil. 2:5 Let this mind be in you
Phil. 3:15 As are mature, have this mind
Phil. 4:7 Will guard your heart and mind
Phil. 4:7 (AMP) Peace of God will guard over your spirit and mind
Col. 3:12 Humility of mind and more
2 Thess. 2:2 (NASB) Not shaken in mind
2 Tim. 1:7 (AMP) God hath given us the spirit of sound mind (self-discipline)
Heb. 8:10 Put my law (word) into their mind
1 Pet. 1:3 Gird up the loins of your mind
1 Pet. 4:1 Same attitude or mind
2 Pet. 3:1 Be in obedience to God's word, for you are his bride (key)
Rev. 17:9 Mind that has wisdom

Matt. 22:37 (AMP) Love God with heart (spirit), soul, mind
Mark 12:30 Love God with all your mind
Luke 10:37 Love—with all your mind
Prov. 23:7 (AMP) He thinks in his heart (as a man)

The mind of God is the mind of Christ, and the Father and Son live in you (me, Bryan).

We cannot have the mind of Christ until we (us, I, me) have been born into His kingdom—adopted into the household of God (His kingdom transformed by His power).

A humble mind, a steadfast mind, a pure mind, a merciful mind—the mind of Jesus Christ is for today and always the same. Happy treasure hunting!

Where there is no word from God, people are uncontrolled.
—Proverbs 29:18 (ICB)

Without revelation, people run wild.
—Proverbs 29:18 (HCSB)

Where there is no vision [no revelation of God and His word], the people are unrestrained.
—Proverbs 29:18 (AMP)

ABOUT THE AUTHOR

All my friends call me Featherchicken. For thirty-seven years with American Airlines. I have had a book business, and I travel to book shows. A retail clothing store. Everything is true—all the stories about me, Featherchicken. This letter is about the Father, not about me. I read and listen and take notes. I'm a treasure hunter for the truth. I dig and dig. The Father said to me, "Take notes, my son. Not all preachers are my anointed." These are my treasure notes that are written about "the power of the Father's word that lives in me, Featherchicken."

Yes, my full name that was from the Father is Evangelist B. D. Featherchicken, at your service. Have Bible, will travel. I have traveled and pan fold from Australia to South Dakota and hunted for the iron door in the Wichita Mountains in Oklahoma. I have walked the beach in Florida with my metal detector, looking for treasure. I have studied antiques and relics and coin collections. I am a jack-of-all-trades yet a master of none. The greatest treasure I have ever found was in Irving, Texas, in my front yard; and that treasure hunt kept growing and growing. Today, I am blessed and highly favored and truly loved. I dig deep in the Father's Word for more of His goodness. His words are like honey in my mouth, and His words feed my spirit so I can pull down strongholds.

Printed in the USA
CPSIA information can be obtained
at www.ICGtesting.com
JSHW011142271123
52342JS00016B/132